Introduction

The South West Coast Path (SWCP), the longest waymarked trail in Britain, runs 630 miles/1014kms around the south west corner of England; starting at Minehead in Somerset then continuing around the coasts of Devon and Cornwall before ending at Poole in Dorset. Over its length the path passes through a great range of landscapes and provides superb walking.

Some walkers may choose to attempt the whole route – a tough undertaking, but one which is made easier by the number of towns and villages providing regular accommodation and supplies along the way. This series of guides, however, provide a different approach, suggesting a number of shorter walks – usually circuits – which can be found on a given stretch of the path. The walks included are relatively short, but all of them can be extended simply by continuing further along the SWCP.

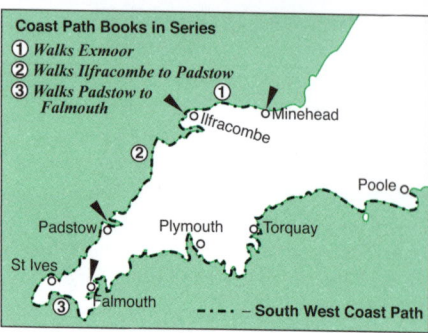

The coastline covered in this guide runs from the picturesque harbour town of Padstow on the Camel estuary *(Walk 1)*, round Land's End – the most westerly point on the English mainland *(9)* – and along the south coast to the town of Falmouth, by its enormous natural harbour *(20)*.

This coastline is very beautiful, and very varied. The estuary of the Camel is a rare intrusion into the northern coast, which typically consists of stretches of cliffs broken up by wide sand beaches (very popular with surfers) backed by extensive areas of dunes – notably at Holywell *(4)* and at Hayle, behind St Ives Bay *(3)*. The south coast is very different, with sunken valleys providing a number of sea inlets winding into the farmland, notably at Falmouth *(20)*, the Helford River *(18,19)* and Porthleven, where one such inlet has been cut off from the sea by the dramatic shingle mound of Loe Bar *(13)*.

The tough granite of the Land's End peninsula provides further high cliffs *(6,7,8,9)*, and given the frequency with which such cliffs will be met on these walks it is worth making a general point. Sea cliffs are one of the great attractions of the SWCP, but also its greatest danger. Please take great care when walking near the cliff tops – particularly in windy conditions – and be aware of the danger of rock falls. Sections of the path can be washed away and you must follow any directions shown on the ground. For advance warning of any problems, it is worth checking on **www.southwestcoastpath.com** – a useful source of information on all aspects of the route.

The stretch of coast covered by this guide is entirely within the county of Cornwall, and visitors will often see the Cornish flag –

a white cross on a black background – either on souvenirs or flying from buildings. This is the cross of St Piran: the patron saint of tin miners. Cornwall has been associated with mining for many centuries, and reminders of the heyday of the county's tin mining will be encountered on a number of walks; notably the

The Cross of St Piran – the Cornish Flag

quarries, spoil heaps and ruined pump houses around St Agnes *(5)* and Botallack *(8)*, which date from the industry's peak in the late 19th/early 20th centuries.

Another geological oddity of Cornwall is serpentine rock. This is only found on the Lizard peninsula *(15,16)*, where souvenirs of the district carved from the stone can be found. The Lizard is also the best place to catch sight of another of Cornwall's most famous symbols. The chough – a crow with a red bill and legs – appears on the county's coat of arms. It had been extinct in the area for several decades until it began breeding again, on the cliffs around the Lizard, in 2001. In recent years it has begun to spread to other sites – generally coastal cliffs – so it is worth keeping your eyes open.

One final symbol of Cornwall is its language – a Celtic language related to Breton and Welsh. The last native Cornish speakers appear to have died by the end of the 19th century – John Davey, buried at Zennor, may have been the last *(7)* – but there has been a revival of interest in the language in recent decades. Visitors may find it useful to get hold of a guide to some to the simpler place name elements to help them understand the landscape – the ubiquitous prefix 'tre-', for instance, means a farm or settlement.

Farming, fishing and mining were the traditional industries in Cornwall, but the county has a more surprising connection with the development of global communications technology. Starting in 1870, the bay at Porthcurno *(11)* was the termination point

A Chough

for the web of undersea telegraph cables linking Britain to the Empire and the rest of the world. Communication with ships was more difficult. In 1872 a signal station (now called the Lloyds Signal Station) was built on the Lizard *(16)*. It would receive semaphore signals from ships arriving in the Channel and send the messages on by telegraph.

Lloyds Signal Station (see Walk 16)

A small hut just along the coast contains the technology which would eventually make this station redundant. This is the oldest surviving Marconi wireless station in its original state, and once set a distance record by receiving a radio signal from the Isle of Wight. Marconi is perhaps better known through his association with Poldhu *(14)*, a little to the north, from where he sent the first transatlantic radio signal in 1901. There is now a small museum near the site.

There are numerous small towns and villages along the coast and inland, but the major service centres are Padstow, Newquay, the picturesque harbour town of St Ives (best known as the home of numerous artists and potters, and now home to the Tate St Ives gallery *(6)*), Penzance (the terminus of the railway and of the ferry to the Isles of Scilly) and Falmouth, plus Redruth and Camborne inland.

Driving in the area is simple enough – as long as you stick to the main roads! As soon as you venture on to the minor roads – as you will need to, to reach many of these walks – things become more complicated. Leave plenty of time for journeys, work out your routes in advance and don't rush on the single-track roads. The area is so beautiful that the journeys to and from the walks are part of the pleasure of the day.

Tate St Ives (see Walk 6)

1 Padstow _____ B

A low-level loop on good paths, starting by broad sands and returning through farmland. Length: **3¹/₂ miles/5.6km**; *Height Climbed:* **330ft/100m**. *Possible link with Walk 2.*

O.S. Sheet 106

Park in Padstow and walk round to the northern side of the harbour (the left-hand side as you look across the River Camel). The road is a dead-end, but just before it ends there is a split. Go left here (Hawker's Cove) and start climbing.

You find yourself on a clear path at the foot of a grassy slope. Shortly after you leave the last houses there is a split, with the right-hand path signposted for the Rock ferry. Keep straight on here.

Just beyond the war memorial there is a gate/stile. The flight of steps to your left is your return route; for now keep straight on, heading towards the mouth of the estuary.

The clear path kinks left around little St George's Cove, then becomes rougher and swings left, along the edge of a field, behind the dunes by the larger Harbour Cove.

The path descends to a junction with a larger track. A diversion to the right at this point leads down to the sands at the head of the cove (or, ¹/₂ mile/0.8km along the Coast Path, to a link with Walk 2. To complete this circuit, however, go left.

The track climbs to the left of Tregirls Farm. Level with the end of the buildings you cross a stile and continue down the driveway ahead.

Keep straight on until the road narrows, you enter trees and there are

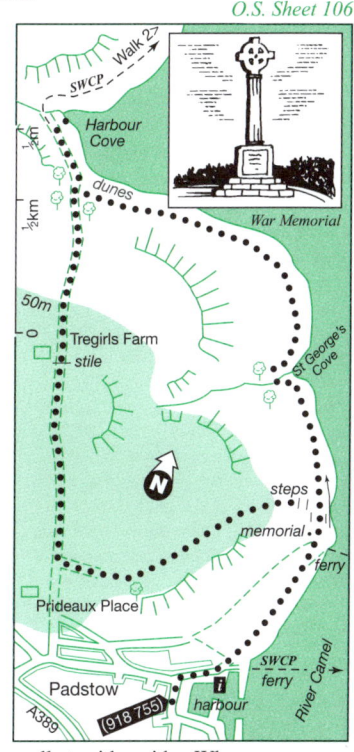

walls to either side. When you can see the roofs of Prideaux Place ahead-right, watch for a lane starting to your left, between walls.

Follow the clear path out of the trees then along field edges to return to the war memorial.

2 Trevone   B

A rough path around a headland providing stunning cliff scenery. Part of the route is along a quiet public road. Length: **5½ miles/8.8km**; Height Climbed: **490ft/150m**. *Possible link with Walk 1.*

Trevone is a village about a mile/1.6km west of Padstow on the B3276. Drive down through the village and park in the small car park behind the narrow beach.

Follow the track around the head of the bay, and when it heads off to the right, towards the buildings at Porthmissen, continue on a rougher path along the coast.

The path runs round the grassy area on Roundhole Point (the 'Round Hole' itself – a collapsed sea cave – is visible on the slope); climbing to a corner of walls. Continue along the coast beyond, enjoying the extraordinary cliff formations.

The path drops to cross a narrow valley. Climb the far side and continue for a short distance to reach a wall with a signpost on the near side. Go right here (yellow arrow) and follow the wall a short distance to join the narrow public road. Turn left.

Follow this road for a mile/1.6km to the houses at Hawker's Cove. A turn to the right at this point will allow you to link with Walk 1, via the Coast Path. For this route, however, follow the signs for Stepper Point through the houses and up to a gate on the far side.

Beyond the gate a clear path runs along the east side of the headland, out to the point. Follow it round the point, past the lookout station and

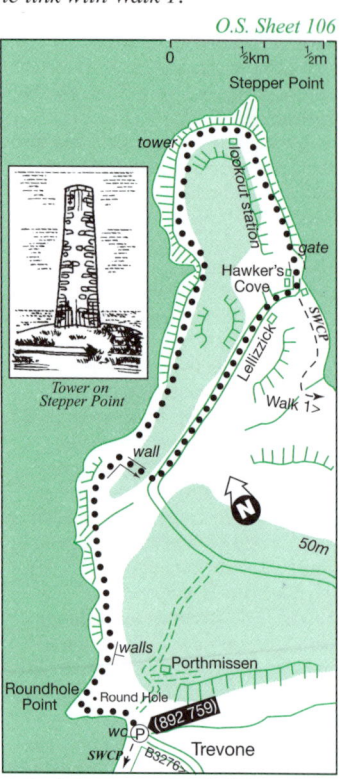

Tower on Stepper Point

O.S. Sheet 106

on to the stone tower – built as a navigation mark for boats approaching Padstow.

Beyond the tower the path runs clear, along the cliffs, back to Trevone.

3 Hayle _____ B

A moderate loop past a fine garden, down a narrow estuary and through dunes behind a wide sand beach. Length: **3½ miles/5.6km**; *Height Climbed:* **165ft/50m**.

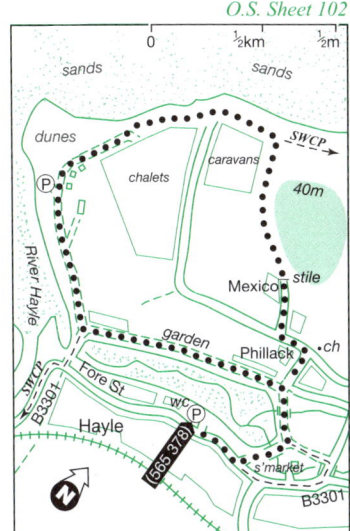

O.S. Sheet 102

Hayle is a small town just east of St Ives. The car park is between the main street (Fore St/B3301) and the narrow tidal bay.

Come out of the car park and turn left (east) along the street. When buildings start to both sides of the road a sign points left for a footpath. Walk down between shops to reach a footbridge over a stream (**NB:** this may not be passable at high tide. If this is the case, continue along Fore St to the road bridge – *see* map).

At a junction with a track turn left and follow the track over a bridge to reach a junction with a metalled road on the far side of the bay.

Turn left, by the bay, following a cinder track running parallel to the road with a fine subtropical garden to your right. When the garden ends turn right, down the road beside the narrow Hayle Estuary.

When the road splits keep left. This leads to a car park. It is worth walking to the front of the car park to see the view over the sands to St Ives, but for the walk go right, following a line of beach huts and chalets.

As the metalled road begins to turn right a sign points left for the Coast Path. Follow the path through the dunes, past the last of the houses and then a caravan site.

When the caravans end a yellow arrow points ahead-right. Turn off the Coast Path here and follow a path through the grass-covered dunes, roughly parallel to the edge of the caravan site.

The path passes beneath a line of pylons and the houses of Mexico become visible ahead. Aim just inside the left-hand edge of the houses (there are a number of paths) to reach a stile. Edge to the left beyond the stile to join a metalled road with the houses to your right.

Turn left at the junction with the road, then right at a junction by a church, to return to the bay.

4 Holywell_____B

A circuit through extensive sand dunes, across grazing land and past beaches and low cliffs. Some care needed with navigation. Length:
4½ miles/7km; *Height Climbed:* undulating.

O.S. Sheet 104

Holywell is a small resort village just south of Newquay. Follow the A3075 2 miles south from the edge of Newquay then turn right onto a minor road. Drive through the village then follow the road left to reach the National Trust car park.

Walk back to the complex junction in the village. Go left, on the near side of the shop. Almost immediately there is a split. Keep right, by the houses.

This section of the route is difficult to describe in detail: there is a large area of dunes ahead with a lot of paths running through it. Swing right, following the line of houses. When these end, continue with the golf course over a fence to your right.

The path climbs to a kissing-gate in a fence. Go through that and continue by the golf course, with the boundary fence heading a little to the right. This quickly leads you to the top corner of the golf course.

When the golf course ends a wall runs straight on from the corner, with a gate in it to your right. Go through this and keep walking in the same direction, now with the wall to your left and open grassland to your right.

Follow the wall while it runs straight. When it bends away to the left keep straight on along a clear path. This descends into a shallow, grassy valley then climbs the far slope to join a grassy track, running right to left. Turn left along the track.

This descends, through pleasant grassland, towards a valley running right to left ahead. Just before you reach it there is a split, with one path heading left to a gate. This is the start of a possible shorter version of this walk (*see* map), but for the longer route keep to the right, bending round towards the houses at Treago Mill.

You pass the entrance to a camp site to your left. Immediately to the right of the gate a path starts, between a wall and a fence. Follow this across a wooden footbridge over the stream and up to a metalled road beyond. Turn left along the road, away from the houses.

Follow the access road up to the village of West Pentire. Turn left at the junction (Porth Joke Beach) and walk past a house and a hotel to reach a gate at the entrance to Pentire Point. A short way beyond there is a signposted junction; go straight on. After 40 paces there is a second junction. This time go right (Crantock).

Walk down the slope, between fields, with a fine view ahead of the sands of Crantock Beach and Newquay beyond. Above the shore you join the Coast Path. Go left, through a gate.

After a short distance there is a signposted split. A short detour to the right will lead to rocky Vugga Cove with (tides allowing) the sands below. Then return to the main path and continue along the coast.

Walk around Pentire Point West and double back, up the side of narrow Porth Joke with its long tongue of sand. Cross a footbridge at the head of the bay, beyond which there is a three-way junction. Go ahead (Holywell), and follow the path round Kelsey Head and back towards the sands of Holywell Bay, with Gull Rocks offshore.

Shortly before you reach the dunes you go through a gate, beyond which the path splits. If you go left you return to the edge of the golf course and can retrace your steps from there. If you go right you have to find a way back to the start via the dunes or the beach.

5 St Agnes   A

A complex circuit leading along cliff tops to one of the classic Cornish views – the chimneys at Wheal Coates – then returning over a low hill. Care will be needed on the cliffs and with navigation. Length:
5½ miles/8.8km; *Height Climbed:* **820ft/250m**.

O.S. Sheet 104

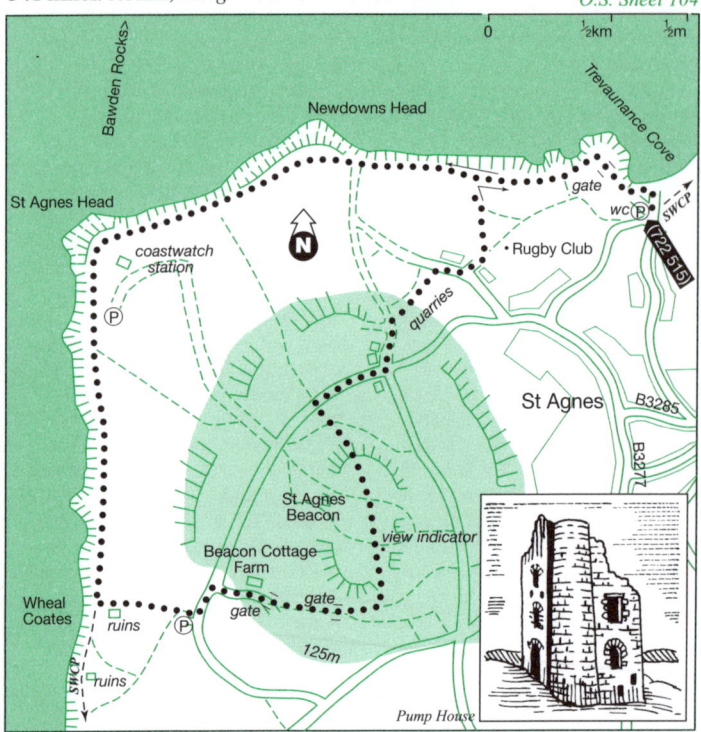

St Agnes is a small town 6 miles north of Redruth by the A30 and B3277. Its economy was traditionally based on tin and copper mining, and there is a mass of industrial relics along the coast, including the towering engine houses at Wheal Coates.

From the centre of the town follow the signs for the beach. This leads you down a narrow valley to a car park behind the sandy beach at Trevaunance Cove.

Walk down towards the beach. Just before you reach it a flight of steps climbs to your left. This climbs to the Jubilee Walk, which runs along the coast. You start along a tarmac road between houses. Where these end there is a gate, beyond which you are on a track, gradually deteriorating to a rough path.

Ignore paths heading inland and continue along the cliff top, past the first spoil heaps and chimneys of the old mining industry. Offshore is the rocky stack of Bawden Rocks.

After a little over a mile/1.6km you pass the Coastwatch Station at St Agnes Head and the path follows the coast due south. You quickly pass a small car park, up to your left, and the mine buildings of Wheal Coates and Towanroath, clinging to the slope above the sea, become visible ahead.

Walk on down to the buildings – maintained by the National Trust – and explore them. This was a tin mine, and the structures were built between 1872 and 1913, when the mine was closed. The tall buildings with chimneys attached housed the pump engines – steam engines which pumped water from the deep shafts.

Turn left (inland) from the first group of buildings and a clear track leads up to a car park. Join the road beyond this and turn left. After around 100m a driveway opens up to the right (Beacon Cottage Farm). Follow this metalled track through the camp site and then the farm buildings beyond (avoid the bits marked 'private' and you won't go wrong).

At the end of the buildings there is a large double gate. Go left on the near side of this to reach a gate and a signpost. Walk across the field beyond (keep out of the way of any grazing animals) in the direction indicated, latterly with a wall to your left, to reach a gate/stile leading on to St Agnes Beacon.

There are numerous paths on the hill. Just aim to climb to the top (where there are fine views in all directions and a view indicator to annotate them) then walk on along the ridge (ie, northwards, towards the sea).

Ignore paths heading right and follow this strip of moorland down to the road, joining it where fields encroach from the right. At this point Bawden Rocks are almost directly ahead of you.

Turn right along the road for a short distance to reach a junction in a group of houses. Go left (byway) on a track which curves to the right in the houses then to the left after it leaves them. Almost immediately after the second curve a footpath heads off to the right.

Turn off the track onto the footpath and follow it through overgrown spoil heaps and quarries. Keep left at the one significant junction and join the public road opposite the entrance to Polberro House. Turn right along the road then take the second track to the left (path to Coast Path).

At the next junction go left to rejoin the Coast Path, then turn right to return to the start.

6 St Ives _____ B

A short section of the tough cliff walk west from St Ives – along the town waterfront and a stretch of cliff top. There is a possible return through fields, but this should not be attempted without an OS Map. Length: **4½ miles/7km** *(there and back); Height Climbed:* **395ft/120m**.

O.S. Sheet 102

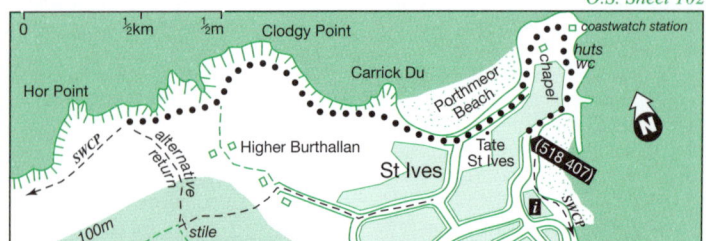

Walk north around the harbour in St Ives (ie, if you are facing the sea head left). From the far end of the bay follow the signs for the Coast Path. They lead you to a small beach with bathing huts. Walk past them and climb the steps beyond.

Pass inside the Coastwatch Station and continue round the headland, passing below the little St Nicholas Chapel. At the next beach – Porthmeor – follow the signs off the beach and through the streets behind it; passing the Tate St Ives gallery on the way.

You reach a small car park to the right and the road swings left. Edge right, through the car park, to reach the start of the path beyond the town.

Follow the clear path past the little Carrick Du headland, by the end of the beach, then onto the cliffs of Clodgy Point. The path goes round the headland (follow the signs) then inland to pass round the head of a rocky gully. There is a signposted junction here: continue along the coast.

If you have no OS map, continue as far as you wish then double back.

If you have a map, continue for a short distance then take a path up to the left, towards a wall. (If you are drawing level with Hor Point, with the rocks off its end, you have gone too far and should double back.) This should lead you to a signposted junction, with the Coast Path forward and back and a footpath heading inland between walls.

Follow this track for ¼ mile/ 0.4km, through a patchwork of small fields, until it turns to the left and there is a signposted four-way junction. Go left, over a stile, and follow the right of way through dense undergrowth then a sequence of fields (virtually impossible without a map) to reach a narrow public road. Follow this back into St Ives.

7 Zennor_____C

A short circuit from a picturesque village to the cliffs and back. Length:
2 miles/3.2km; *Height Climbed:* **165ft/50m**.

O.S. Sheet 102

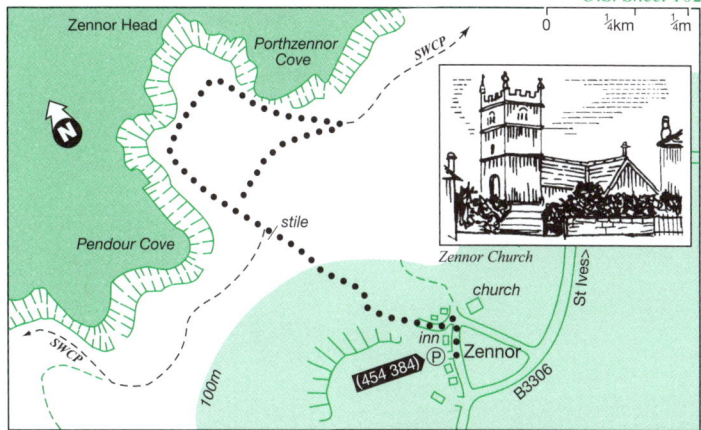

The tiny village of Zennor, with its inn and fine old church, is 5 miles west of the centre of St Ives along the B3306. Turn off onto a minor road and park in the car park.

Walk north towards the church (Norman in part, and with a monument in the churchyard to John Davey Jr – one of the last native speakers of Cornish – who died in 1891). Keep to the left of the church. The road quickly forks: keep left here (Coast Path).

A metalled road leads past houses, and when the road stops you continue on a clear path. Cross a stone stile and there is a signposted split, with the Coast Path going in both directions. Obviously you can follow the winding, undulating cliff-top path in either direction for as far as you wish. For this short walk, go right.

When the wall to your right ends a path heads off to the right. That is your return route; for now, keep straight on. The path runs straight, with Pendour Cove down to the left, then curves right around the end of Zennor Head.

The path then drops down towards the head of Porthzennor Cove before climbing again to a junction by a wall. Turn right to return to the junction by the stile then retrace your steps to the start.

On a general note, the field paths behind the cliffs should be avoided unless you have a detailed map or already know the area – navigation is very difficult.

8 Botallack _____ B

*A short, steep circuit exploring dramatic ruins of buildings connected with the tin mining industry. Fine cliff scenery; path steep in places.
Length:* **3 miles/4.8km**; *Height Climbed:* **260ft/80m**. *Great care should be taken when exploring the old sites – particularly when looking at the Crowns Mine pump houses, on their cliff-edge site.*

O.S. Sheet 102

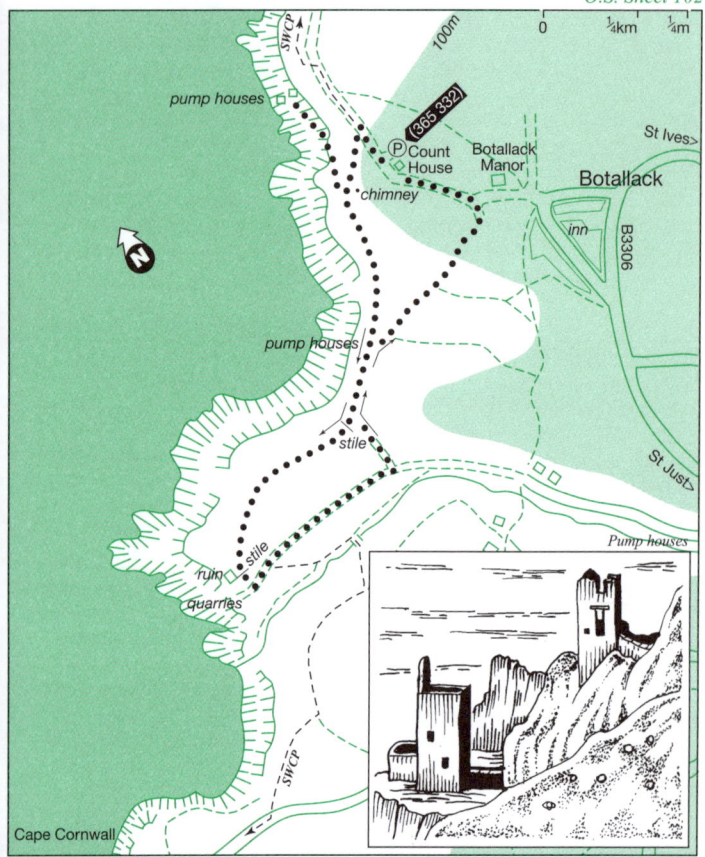

Botallack is a small village in the heart of the old tin mining area at the far west end of Cornwall. The area is littered with old pits, spoil heaps and pump houses. This walk passes two of the most dramatic ruins.

Botallack is 6 miles north of Land's End along the A30/B3306. Turn into the village and drive to the north end, where the road bends right to rejoin the B3306. Rather than following the road, keep straight on along a clear track. This bends left (at Botallack Manor) then quickly splits. Keep right and drive on a short way to pass the old Count House to your right. The car park is immediately beyond.

The Count House was built in the 1860s as the office for the mines, which were closed in 1914. The area is now managed by the National Trust.

Walk out of the car park and continue along the track. Shortly after passing a large metal structure (headgear for the mine) to your right you reach a milestone for the Coast Path. Take the path heading back-left, downhill. Immediately below a tall chimney there is a second junction, with a path heading back-right. Turn on to that and follow it down and across the slope to the old Crowns Mine pump houses.

The cliff-edge site is highly dramatic. Please take extreme care when looking at the buildings, then double back to the junction below the chimney.

Keep straight on at the junction. You are now on the Coast Path and climb gently to pass two further pump houses before reaching a junction. A path goes back-left for Botallack. That is your return route, but for now keep on along the coast.

Shortly beyond there is a further signposted junction. This time go right (Cape Cornwall). The path quickly crosses a stile over a wall and continues out along the little peninsula – once the site of an Iron Age fort but now with only the ruin of a mine building.

Admire the view south to Cape Cornwall then descend to your left from the ruin to find a stone stile. Note the warning notice here: there is an old quarry beyond the stile and you must stick to the path.

The rough path descends to join the old access track to the quarry. Turn left along this, up the side of a valley. After a short distance there is a signposted junction. The Coast Path heads right at this point, down into the valley, but for this short walk keep straight on (Tregeseal).

After $1/4$ mile/0.4km you reach an unsignposted junction, with a clear track heading back-left. Turn on to this and follow it across the neck of the headland then back to the junction by the two pump houses.

This time keep straight on (Botallack). The track heads inland between fields (there are two signposted junctions; keep straight on at both – red arrow). When you join the original access road turn left to return to the car park by the Count House.

Walks Padstow to Falmouth

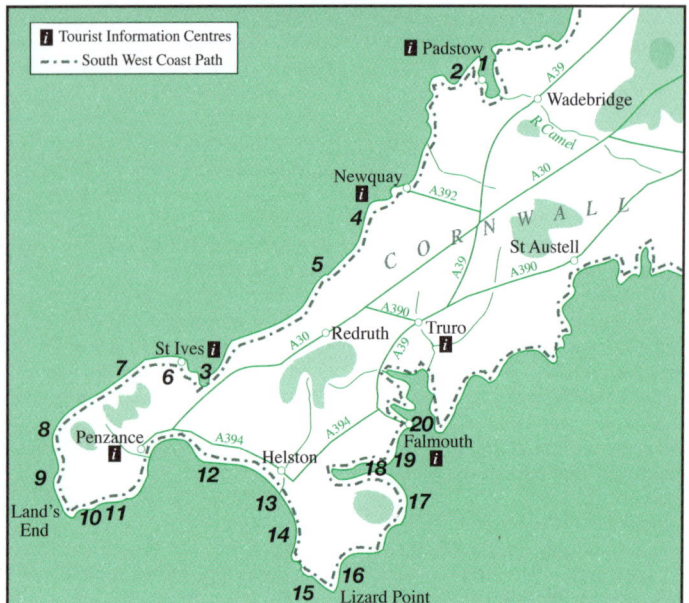

Grades

A ...... Strong walking footwear and waterproof clothing required. Conditions wet or rough and care needed with navigation.

B ...... Strong walking footwear and waterproof clothing required. Underfoot conditions generally good and navigation largely straightforward.

C ...... Comfortable walking footwear recommended.

— www.pocketwalks.com —

Published by: Hallewell Publications, The Milton, Foss, Pitlochry PH16 5NQ
Printed by: J Thomson Printers, Glasgow

While every care has been taken in the preparation of this guide, the publishers cannot accept responsibility for any loss, damage or injury resulting from its use.

Walks Padstow to Falmouth

walk	grade
1 Padstow	B
2 Trevone	B
3 Hayle	B
4 Holywell	B
5 St Agnes	A
6 St Ives	B
7 Zennor	C
8 Botallack	B
9 Sennen Cove & Land's End	B
10 Porthgwarra	B
11 Porthcurno & Penberth	A
12 Prussia Cove	C
13 Loe Bar	B
14 Poldhu Cove & Mullion	B
15 Kynance Cove	B
16 The Lizard	A
17 Porthallow	A
18 Helford & Frenchman's Creek	B
19 Rosemullion Head	B
20 Pendennis Point	C

9 Sennen Cove & Land's End _____ B

A circuit starting at a small harbour, climbing to the Land's End cliffs, then returning inland. Steep in places. Length: **3 miles/4.8km**; *Height Climbed:* **230ft/70m**.

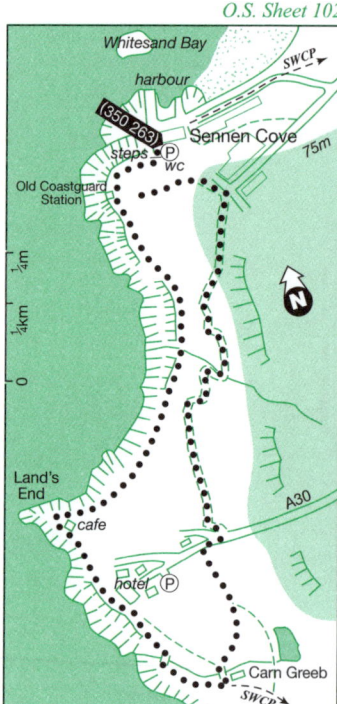

O.S. Sheet 102

Land's End needs no introduction; Sennen Cove is the harbour village immediately to the north, by the sands of Whitesand Bay. Obviously there is parking at Land's End, but this walk is described starting from Sennen Cove – so that you make the climb onto the cliffs at the start of the walk.

Park in the car park behind the harbour. Walk past the toilet block and turn left at the sign for the Coast Path; passing between houses, climbing a flight of steps beyond, then heading right, across the slope, to the old Coastguard Station.

The path beyond is straightforward; along the cliffs to the mass of gift shops and cafes at the most westerly point of mainland England. Pass in front of the hotel and continue along the coast, aiming for a building with 'crafts' written on it.

Having looked at the crafts, cross the bridge over the little stream beside the building. Immediately, a blue arrow points ahead-right, up a rough footpath. Follow this path – keeping ahead-left at the one signposted junction – to join the access road to Land's End.

Turn right along the road for about 80 paces. Just after a second road joins from the left a track heads off left, signposted for Sennen Cove. Follow this clear track all the way back to a junction with a public road by the first houses of Sennen Cove.

At this complex junction two tracks head left immediately. Take the nearer of the two. Follow it downhill until it turns sharp right. At that point keep straight on along a footpath leading straight down to the old Coastguard Station.

10 Porthgwarra _____ B

A short cliff-top circuit, starting from a tiny village with a small beach. Superb cliff scenery. Length: **2½ miles/4km**; *Height Climbed:* **430ft/130m**.

O.S. Sheet 102

Excavated shelter behind beach

Porthgwarra is a tiny village; a handful of houses and a cafe at the mouth of a small valley. It has a narrow beach between cliffs and a tunnel, dug by tin miners, to give access to the shore. To reach the village, drive 2½ miles east from Land's End on the B3315, then turn south on a minor road.

Park in the car park and walk back towards the shore. You quickly reach a signposted junction. For this walk you will go right (Land's End), but it is worth walking on a short way to look at the tunnel and the excavated shelter behind the beach.

The path climbs on to the cliffs and bends around Hella Point and Gwennap Head, passing two cones (shipping marks for a rock offshore) and a Coastwatch Station. Care must be taken on the cliffs, but the weathered rocks are superb.

Go through a gate in a wall, noting the view of the hotel at Land's End ahead, with the lighthouse offshore. The path runs round a further headland then begins to descend to cross a stream. Double back at this point. There are a number of paths through the moorland behind the cliffs; find one which aims for the gap in the wall inland from the cliffs.

This should put you on a track heading towards a house below and to the left of the Coastwatch Station. Join a metalled road by the house and follow it back to the car park.

11 Porthcurno & Penberth ─────────── A

A complex circuit linking two coastal villages, with a diversion to an open air theatre. Superb cliff scenery. **Length: 4½ miles/7km**; *Height Climbed:* **820ft/250m**. *Steep undulations along the coast section.*

O.S. Sheet 102

Porthcurno is a tiny coastal village 3 miles east of Land's End by the B3315 and a minor road. Although small, the village has two claims to fame. First, there is an open air theatre on the cliffs to the west of the bay; and second, between 1870 and 1970 Porthcurno was the landing point for underwater telegraph cables carrying information from overseas. Information on the latter activities can now be found in the Porthcurno Telegraph Museum.

Park in the car park. From the front of the car park walk on down towards the sand beach. Just before the beach there is a complex junction of paths. The circuit will be starting to the left, but for the diversion to the theatre go right.

The path starts level, on the slope above the beach with a fine view to the rocky Logan Rock headland, before climbing steeply on stone steps to reach the entrance to the theatre. The visitor centre, shop and coffee shop are open April-September.

Return to the junction behind the beach and take the Coast Path to Penberth, climbing the slope beside the beach. At the top of the slope the path makes a loop off to the right before heading inland to reach a T-junction. Go right here and continue along the cliff top.

After $1/2$ mile you reach a junction of paths at the neck of the Logan Rock headland. It is worth making a diversion along the headland – which has a famous rocking stone near its end – but then return to the main path and continue.

Within a short distance you begin a steep descent to the little village of Penberth – one of the few fishing villages in Cornwall where you may still see the small, open boats being hauled up the slipway.

As you enter the village go left, on the near side of a stream. You quickly pass to the right of a house. Beyond this, ignore the entrances to an allotment area and continue until you reach a three-way junction. Go left here, uphill through trees.

The rough path goes uphill for a short distance then heads right, across the slope. This leads you to a stile leading into a field. Walk up the right-hand edge of the field, then a few paces to the left at the corner to reach the next stile.

In the second field, walk up the left-hand side. When the wall pulls away head ahead-left, to a gap where there was once a gate.

In the third field walk up the left-hand side. After a few paces there is a stile to your left. Cross this and continue with the wall to your right. At the corner of this field turn left and continue between fences.

You approach a house, but cross a stile to your right just before it. The path beyond leads in to the village of Treen. Turn left in the village and follow the track out towards the camp site.

At the entrance to the camp site turn left, on a clear track. Follow this back down to the Coast Path and turn right to return to the start.

12 Prussia Cove — C

A very short loop passing dramatic coves and giving a fine view of St Michael's Mount. Length: **1½ miles/2.4km**; *Height Climbed:* **165ft/50m**.

O.S. Sheet 102

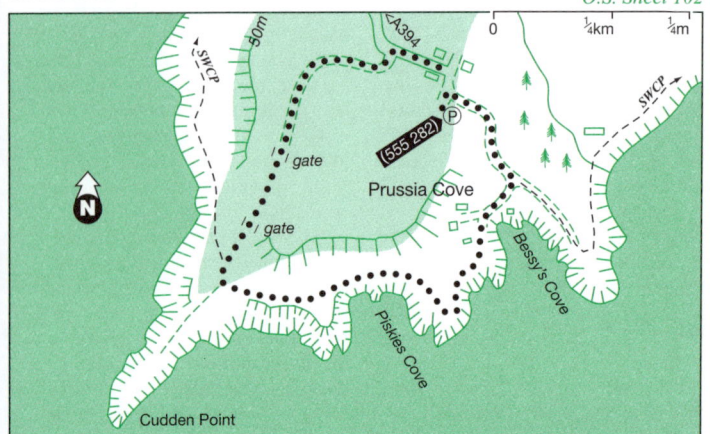

Prussia Cove is a cluster of houses above a string of rocky coves, in an area historically associated with smuggling. To reach it, drive 5 miles east from Penzance on the A30/A394 then turn onto a minor road. After a mile this road ends at the car park.

Walk back out of the car park and turn right (ie, you are walking along a clear track with the car park to your right). When the track reaches a triangular junction turn right.

You quickly pass a house entrance to your right. Keep straight on, passing to the left of a little thatched cottage and continuing on a rough path above Bessy's Cove.

Wind round the little headland then round the back of Piskies Cove and the long headland of Cudden Point becomes visible ahead. Climb on to the ridge of the headland and you get a fine view west to St Michael's Mount, with the castle on its summit, and Penzance and Mousehole beyond.

Turn right on the path running up the ridge through gorse. This leads you to a kissing-gate, beyond which you continue along the bottom of a field.

Follow the field edge and you quickly reach a gate at the bottom of a lane. Follow the lane up to the public road and turn right to return to the start of the walk.

13 Loe Bar   B

A cliff path to the shingle mound of Loe Bar, plus a loop through farmland. Paths generally good. **Length: 3½ miles/5.6km**; **Height Climbed: 260ft/80m**. *Paths pass through grazing fields.*

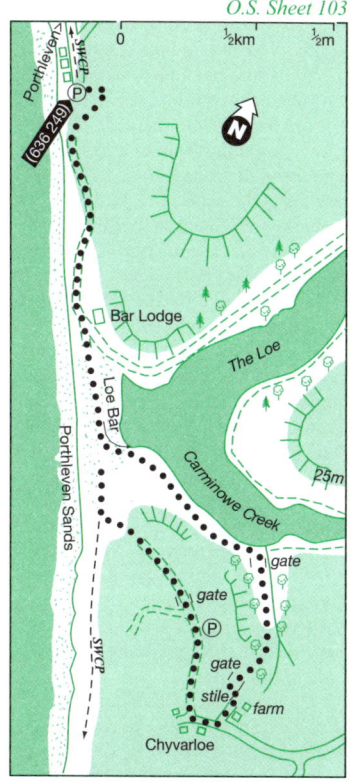

O.S. Sheet 103

Loe Bar is a dramatic geological feature: a long bar of sand and shingle pushed into the mouth of a river valley by wind and tide, creating a large freshwater lake. The easiest approach is from Porthleven – 2 miles west of Helston on the B3304. The coast road to Loe Bar is signposted from the approach to the village.

Park in the car park at the end of the road. From the back of the car park a path zig-zags onto the cliff top and starts along the coast.

In ½ mile/0.8km you pass Bar Lodge. Descend to the Bar and walk across it. On the far side a path starts to your left, along the side of Carminowe Creek.

After ½ mile/0.8km there is a gate to the right (if you cross a stream you have missed it), where there is a sign for Chyvarloe Farm. Go through the gate and head for another, visible ahead-left. Continue up the wooded valley beyond.

At the top of the wood there is a gate. Head half-left beyond this (yellow arrow) to reach a stile over a fence with a stile over a wall just beyond, leading into the buildings at Chyvarloe (National Trust).

Turn right, and at a junction amongst the buildings go right again. You are now on a clear track between fields. At one point it widens to make a small car park, and shortly beyond there is a gate. Just before the gate a track heads off to the left. Ignore that and keep straight on to rejoin the Coast Path. Turn right to return to the start.

14 **Poldhu Cove & Mullion** _____ B

A short cliff-top circuit starting from a fine sand beach and passing sites relating to Marconi and early wireless. **Length: 3 miles/4.8km**; **Height Climbed: 165ft/50m**.

O.S. Sheet 103

The village of Mullion is 6 miles south of Helston by the A3083/B3296. Poldhu Cove is ½ mile north of Mullion on a minor road. Park in the car park behind the wide beach.

Walk out the front of the car park and turn left along the road. Almost immediately a metalled road heads off to the right, along the southern side of the cove. As you approach a large white building a path starts to the right, signposted for the Coast Path.

Follow this path behind the cliff edge, quickly passing a large monument to the first transatlantic wireless transmission – sent from Marconi's Poldhu Wireless Station to St John's, Newfoundland, in 1901.

The path remains clear until it passes through a gap in a wall and splits. The Coast Path follows the right-hand path, down to Polurrian Cove, visible below. For this circuit, however, keep to the left, following the top of the slope round to join an access road and continuing up the side of the valley.

On the outskirts of Mullion you draw level with a post box and a sign points ahead-left for a footpath. After a short distance you edge left into a paddock, the route across which is marked by posts.

On the far side, go through a narrow band of woodland with a stile at either side. Beyond this you are in another narrow field (please avoid any grazing animals). Aim just to the right of a large stone house to reach a gate on to a lane. Turn left along this, with the house to your left and a thatched cottage to your right.

Follow this clear track back to the large white building, on the near side of which is the Marconi Centre, providing information about the wireless station.

Follow the access track down to the metalled road and retrace your steps to the car park.

15 Kynance Cove _____ B

A cliff-top circuit passing a cafe at the head of a narrow cove. Fine cliff scenery of particular geological interest. Length: **3½ miles/5.6km**; *Height Climbed:* **490ft/150m**.

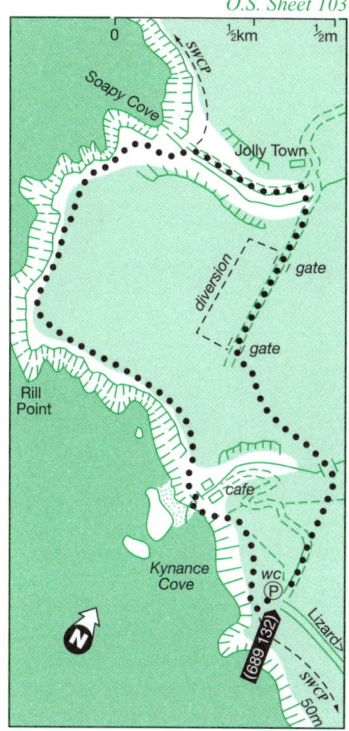

O.S. Sheet 103

Kynance Cove has long been known for its splendid cliff scenery, and for its serpentine rock formations. Serpentine, which is peculiar to the area, is carved locally to make souvenirs.

To reach the cove, turn west onto a minor road just north of the village of Lizard (*see* Walk 16). This leads to a National Trust car park.

Take the viewpoint path from the front of the car park then turn right along the cliffs. You quickly join the main path from the car park: turn left to descend to the cafe. (**NB:** this involves walking below the high water mark; if this is not possible, take the diversion signposted.)

Cross the stream by the cafe and turn left; climbing steeply to the cliff top and continuing on a clear path. This runs west to Rill Point then turns north before descending to the valley above the beach at Soapy Cove.

Cross the stream and turn right, up the valley, on an old track. When you draw level with the house at Jolly Town, up to your left, recross the stream to join a clear track. Turn right along this, climbing.

The track forms an 'S' then runs straight to reach a gate (ignore the track starting to the right). Walk straight through the enclosed fields ahead (if you wish to avoid grazing animals, you can make a diversion to the right of the walled area).

At the far end there are two gates and two signposted paths. Go left and follow a path through heather and gorse to a footbridge over a stream. Beyond this there are a number of paths: pick one which heads for the car park, visible ahead.

16 The Lizard

A circuit around the cliffs of the headland with possible shorter options (see map). Paths are generally good but there are short, steep climbs in places and care must be taken on the cliffs. Length: up to **5 miles/8km**; *Height Climbed:* undulating.

O.S. Sheet 10.

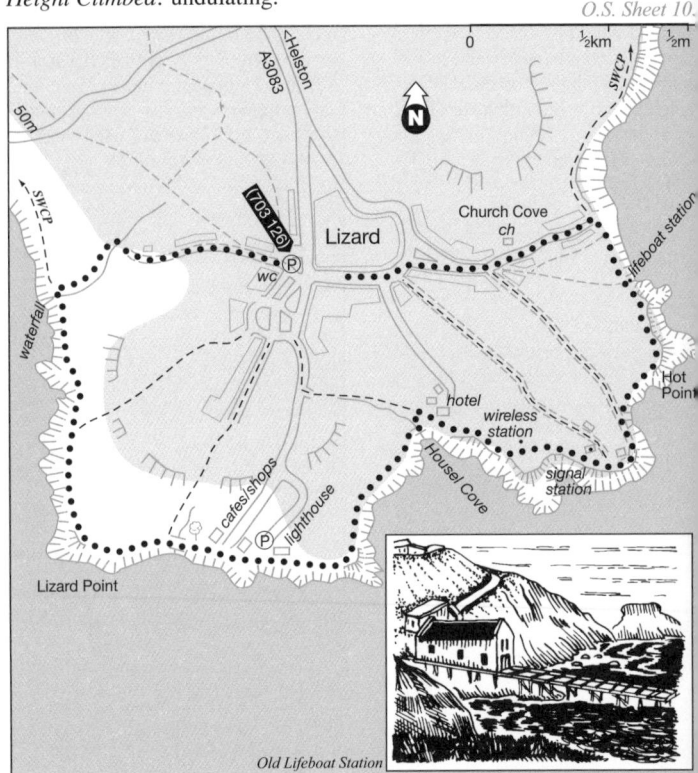

Old Lifeboat Station

The Lizard peninsula is the most southerly point of the British mainland. The village of Lizard sits in the middle of the headland with paths radiating to the coast like wheel spokes. This walk runs round the entire southern part of the headland, but there are several opportunities to shorten the route (*see* map).

To reach Lizard, drive south from Helston on the A3083. There is a car park by the lighthouse, but for this walk park in the larger car park in Lizard itself.

From the centre of the village, take the road which passes to the right of the public conveniences and follow it out of the village. You quickly reach a signposted split, with a path heading off ahead-right. Ignore this and keep straight on along the bridleway.

Follow this clear track past the last of the houses then downhill – the track now a rough path – into a small valley. Cross the stream at the foot of the slope and walk down the valley, with the stream to your left.

At the bottom of the valley you join the Coast Path. Turn left, down steps, to ford the stream just above a small waterfall dropping to Caerthillian Cove.

Beyond this, the route is straightforward for about a mile/1.6km; following the coast south to Lizard Point then heading east towards the lighthouse and old lifeboat station, visible ahead. Shortly before you reach the road-end you descend to a little valley with willow trees, cross a footbridge and climb up the far side to the cafes and craft shops.

Continue along the cliff top beyond, keeping your eye open for choughs – a species of crow with a red beak and feet: the emblem of Cornwall but now rare. The path passes beneath the lighthouse then turns north-east before descending steeply into a narrow valley. Cross the stream on a concrete footbridge. Just beyond, a diversion to the right leads to a small sand beach; otherwise go left, up the valley.

At the top of a flight of steps there is a junction. Go right (yellow arrow) to continue round the coast. On the next stretch you pass the Lizard Wireless Station (the oldest Marconi station to survive in its original state – manned by National Trust volunteers and open to the public) and the Lloyds Signal Station (built in the 19th century to receive signals from passing ships). Be sure to pass outside the Signal Station to continue round the coast.

Beyond the buildings on the point you are on an access track. Follow this for a short distance until a yellow arrow points right and you continue on a grassy footpath on the slope above the sea.

The path rounds Hot Point and passes above the splendid new lifeboat station, more than 200 steps down to your right at Kilcobben Cove. The station is generally open to visitors between 10am and 3.30pm, though it may be closed at any time when it is in use.

Continue a short distance further along the coast before following the path down to the picturesque settlement at Church Cove. Turn left up the road and follow it back to the start of the walk, passing the splendid St Wynwallow's Church on the way – the most southerly church on the British mainland.

17 Porthallow _____ A

An undulating walk along low cliffs and back through farmland. Some walking on quiet public roads. Length: 4½ miles/7km; Height Climbed: 575ft/175m.

O.S. Sheet 103

Drive south from Helston on the A3083/B3293 to the village of St Keverne. The little village of Porthallow is a mile north of St Keverne on minor roads. Park in the car park at the back of the wide shingle beach.

Walk to the left end (if facing the sea) of the beach and take the path which climbs up to the top of the low cliffs. The path runs past four fields, with a grassy slope down to the right, before crossing a stile to enter a grazing field. Head half-right (keeping out of the way of any grazing animals) to reach a stile at the bottom corner of the field, then continue along a clear path out to the observation post on Nare Point.

Beyond that you follow the access track for the observation post on along the coast. At a wooded valley the track turns inland, but you cross the stream and continue along the coast on a rough footpath.

When you reach the first of the houses around Gillan avoid paths to the left and keep going downhill to reach the head of the bay, with a little rocky headland to your right. Near the head of the bay a blue arrow marks the start of a track up the near side of the valley.

Follow the track up the valley to the farm buildings at Trewarnevas (a working cattle farm; avoid livestock where possible) then on up to join the road at a four-way junction.

Go left (Lestowder). The road dog-legs left and, a short distance beyond, there is a sign pointing right for a footpath (Roskorwell). Walk down the left-hand side of two fields, edging left to join a lane towards the end of the second, to reach the houses at Roskorwell.

Keep straight on down the quiet road beyond to return to the start.

18 Helford & Frenchman's Creek _____B

An undulating, low level circuit starting at a picturesque village and passing a wooded, tidal creek. Paths good, but wet in places. Length: **3½ miles/5.6km**; *Height Climbed:* **430ft/130m**.

O.S. Sheet 103

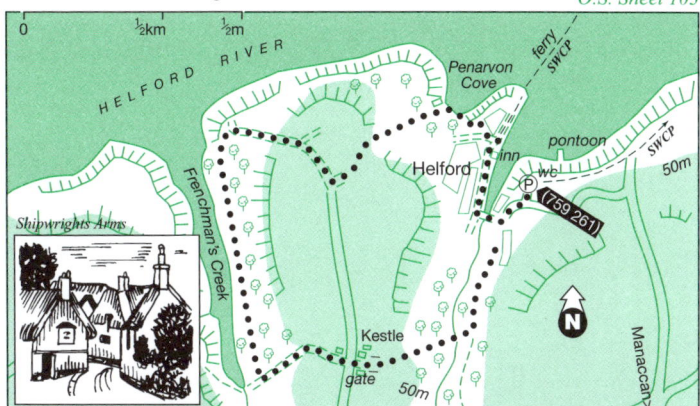

The little village of Helford is not easy to find – just south of Helston, turn off the A3083 onto the B3293. Pass through Garras then follow the signs through the maze of minor roads. Park in the car park.

Walk out of the car park and turn right, descending to cross a footbridge, then turn right, through the village, down the far side of the creek. Immediately beyond the Shipwrights Arms there is a signposted split. A short diversion straight on leads to the ferry (summer only) over the Helford River, but for this walk go back-left.

Turn off right almost immediately (footpath) and follow the path over to Penarvon Cove. Head left, to the head of the cove, where a track heads off to the left (Frenchman's Creek).

Follow this, climbing, until you reach a T-junction. Go right (Frenchman's Creek) on a clear track. When the track enters an arable field and forks go left, by the wall. At the foot of the field the track goes right but you go left (Frenchman's Creek).

Follow a clear, rough path for half a mile/0.8km through the woodland by the narrow, tidal creek. At the top of the creek the path joins a clear track. Turn left and climb to the road.

Walk straight across the road and continue between houses and sheds. At the end of the buildings there are two gates. Go through the right-hand one and follow a path by a field down into a wooded valley. Cross the stream and turn left on a clear (sometimes wet) path, back into Helford.

19 Rosemullion HeadB

A complex circuit, low-level and undulating, along the open coast and through dense woodland, passing a fine old church on the way. Part of the walk is along quiet roads. Length: **4 miles/6.4km**; *Height Climbed:* **330ft/100m**.

O.S. Sheet 103

Lych gate at church

1 *Falmouth* **2** *Pendennis Point & Castle* **3** *St Mawes Castle* **4** *St Mawes* **5** *Carrickmouth Point* **6** *St Anthony Head Point & Lighthouse* **7** *Dodman Point*

The route to the village of Mawnan Smith is not easy to describe, but the village is easy enough to find: it is 2 miles south of Falmouth along minor roads. If you are travelling south through the village, bear left at the junction by the Red Lion Inn, then keep right at a junction beyond the edge of the village, to reach the hamlet of Mawnan at the end of the road. There is a small private car park (honesty box) by the church.

The oldest sections of the church – which sits in a splendid position above the mouth of the Helford River – date back to the 13th century, and the inscription above the lych gate is in Cornish. In translation it means 'it is good for me to draw nigh unto God.'

Walk out of the car park on a clear path, with the church and graveyard to your left. This quickly brings you to a junction with a clear path running along the top of a wooded bank. Turn left.

There is a mass of paths on the slope. Zig-zag down until you are midway down the slope, heading left (north-east) on a clear path through mature, mixed woodland. After descending gradually, through woodland then scrub, you cross a stile and continue along the foot of a field, with a fine view back to your right of the opposite headlands.

Cross three further stiles and you are on Rosemullion Head. Walk around the headland (it is an open access area) then continue along the coast, with a view of Falmouth opening up ahead.

After leaving the headland at a stile/gate you continue through two narrow fields to reach a further gate leading into a wooded area. Cross a stream and you quickly reach a split, with a slipway down to your right. Go left. You quickly join another path and head left, up the strip of woodland.

At the top you go through a gate and turn right along a clear track. This leads you to the public road, where you turn left. Ignore the road heading left for Mawnan Church and continue into Mawnan Smith. Just before the town sign a sign points left for a footpath.

After a short distance the track gets rougher and splits. Go left here (Porth Saxon), down the side of Carwinion Garden (open to the public and notable for its bamboo collection). When the garden ends to your left the path continues down a wooded valley until it reaches the stony beach at Porth Saxon.

Go through a gate on to the shore and turn left. Walk along the back of the beach then climb the slope beyond to reach a gate into a field. Beyond the gate you descend into a little valley (it can be marshy at the bottom). Go through a gate to your right and cross the little stream.

Beyond that you can either turn left and follow a path through fields up to the church, or you can climb into the next field and continue around the coast to return to the church by your original route.

20 Pendennis Point _____C

A short walk around the fortified headland on the eastern edge of Falmouth. Excellent views. **Length: 2 miles/3.2km**; *Height Climbed:* undulating.

O.S. Sheet 103

From the centre of Falmouth follow the signs for the Scenic Route. This takes you out to the one-way system around Pendennis Point. Drive out to the end of the point, where there is a car park.

A quick walk out the front of the car park will lead to the Blockhouse on the point – part of the defences built on the headland by the Tudor monarchs. Pendennis Castle, at the highest point of the hill, was built for Henry VIII in the 1540s.

Double back up the shore (ie, with the car park up to your left) and you will find yourself on the Coast Path, running through woodland with the road up to your left and fine views to your right of the boats in Penryn River and the village of Flushing on the far shore.

The path rejoins the road opposite the entrance to the leisure pool. Cross the road to find the pavement and continue towards Falmouth, with views now opening up of the town, marina and docks.

Follow the road across the neck of the peninsula and on to the junction with the other end of Castle Drive. A diversion to the right at this point will lead down to the centre of Falmouth, but to complete the walk go left; initially through houses, but then with a beach down to the right.

If you want to keep away from the road, watch for a sign for a footpath to the left of the road. This leads to a path through the woods, rejoining the road further on.

Continue along the road to return to the start.